I0469587

THE 21 IRREFUTABLE RULES FOR SELLING IN THE 21ST CENTURY

And Why Your Business Survival Depends On It

JOE KIRDAY

Foreword By
C. William Pollard
Chairman and CEO (Retired)
The ServiceMaster Company

authorHOUSE®

AuthorHouse™
1663 Liberty Drive
Bloomington, IN 47403
www.authorhouse.com
Phone: 1-800-839-8640

First published by AuthorHouse   2/16/2011

ISBN: 978-1-4567-4652-0 (e)
ISBN: 978-1-4567-4653-7 (sc)

Library of Congress Control Number: 2011902929

Printed in the United States of America

Any people depicted in stock imagery provided by Thinkstock are models, and such images are being used for illustrative purposes only. Certain stock imagery © Thinkstock.

This book is printed on acid-free paper.

Contents

Foreword. vii

Endorsements ix

Acknowledgments xi

Introduction xiii

Rule One
    If "No" Bothers You—*Quit!*. *1*

Rule Two
    If You Are Going to Sit, Sit Aggressively 3

Rule Three
    Features Tell—Benefits Sell. 5

Rule Four
    Need-Based Selling Sells. 7

Rule Five
    Value Must Be Perceived for the Sale To Be Received 9

Rule Six
    Sell to the Most Important Customer First—*You!* *11*

Rule Seven
    Learn from Types and Anti-Types. 13

Rule Eight
    Learn How To Tell Time. 15

Rule Nine
    Core Values Are Crucial. 17

Rule Ten
    Stop Whining. 19

Rule Eleven
    Sell Relationships—*Not* Things 21

RULE TWELVE
Get Rid of Your Sales Office 23

RULE THIRTEEN
Sell *Only* on Days That End With a "Y" 25

RULE FOURTEEN
Name-Dropping Is Good 27

RULE FIFTEEN
Know Your Delusions about Communication 29

RULE SIXTEEN
Trust Is *Not* Unbreakable 31

RULE SEVENTEEN
Caveat Venditor—Or—Know Who You Are Selling To 33

RULE EIGHTEEN
Create Gaps Between the Customer's "Haves" and "Wants" . . 35

RULE NINETEEN
By All Means—*Ask* for the Sale 37

RULE TWENTY
Don't Assume the Sale Is Over When the Customer "Buys" . . . 39

RULE TWENTY ONE
There Are Always More Rules 41

CONCLUSION 43
ABOUT THE AUTHOR 49

In business, everything starts with the sale. The sale represents that first step of creating a meaningful relationship with a customer. Without customers, there is no business; there is only activity and a dream. Selling also plays an important role in the process of keeping customers and satisfying their changing and growing needs. Unless a business creates and keeps customers, it will not survive. Selling is all about building relationships of trust.

The lessons to be learned in selling, therefore, are not limited to business. They are also applicable to other areas of life, including developing and growing relationships of trust with our spouses, our children, our friends, and those we seek to serve in our community and in our places of worship.

During the years I served as a senior officer and then Chairman and CEO of ServiceMaster, I had the privilege and opportunity of working with Joe Kirday and seeing him grow as a manager, salesperson, and executive. He knows what it means to make the sale and to develop meaningful relationships of trust with customers. This book reflects the wisdom of someone who not only has the knowledge of selling but also one who has made it happen.

I have also seen Joe grow in his relationship with Christ. It started with that first step of turning to God and accepting His gift of forgiveness and redemptive love. It has continued as Joe's faith has grown in understanding what it means to have a relationship of trust with God.

As you read this book, listen and learn about the art of selling and also reflect upon the importance of developing meaningful and lasting relationships in your life.

C. William Pollard

During the years I served as a senior officer and then Chairman and CEO of ServiceMaster, I had the privilege and opportunity of working with Joe Kirday and seeing him grow as a manager, salesperson, and executive. He knows what it means to "make the sale" and to develop meaningful relationships of trust with customers. This book reflects the wisdom of someone who not only has the knowledge of selling, but also one who has made it happen.

C. William Pollard
Chairman and CEO (Retired)
The ServiceMaster Company

"Over the past twenty-five years I have had the privilege to work with Joe Kirday. Joe has always been an executive within our ServiceMaster organization who can get results and make the sale. In this book, you will learn about the ways that Joe sells with his hands, head, and heart. It is a great book that will give you an opportunity to learn some very powerful tools to make the sale."

Mike Isakson
President and COO
ServiceMaster Franchise Group

Even though I am not officially a sales person, still I learned a lot about the basic principles of selling through reading Joe's delightful book. I believe the principles he puts forward are irrefutable.

Selflessness and a desire to meet the needs of others are basic for all jobs and professions. I heartily recommend this book to all who would like to improve their lives and their bottom line.

Dr. David King (Th.D.)
Pastor and Southern Baptist Missionary to Lebanon

ACKNOWLEDGMENTS

First, I would like to thank Bill Pollard for his willingness to write the foreword to this book. I have known Bill for over thirty-four years, and he had been an inspiration to many new managers within the ServiceMaster Company. When I was in Bill's direct reporting chain, I remember him telling me, "not to ever go to any kind of a meeting unprepared." I carry that advice with me to this day.

No writer ever undertakes the responsibility of writing a book on his own. I am thankful to all individuals and Sales Managers both (Type) and (Anti-Types) who have helped me shape my sales skills and knowledge. To those who helped hone my selling skills, I am eternally grateful. For I know that in all walks of life I will use these skills, both in the secular and spiritual environments.

My thanks go to all who contributed to my growth both the "Types" and the "Anti-Types." My thanks also go to my wife Debbie and my mother-in-law Barbara Elmer who checked my grammar and spelling over and over again prior to sending the book to my publisher.

I am also indebted to Barry Sullivan for his insight and for editing this book. Barry has been a friend of mine for over twenty years and I have learned immensely from his knowledge and wisdom.

I am thankful that Xerox allowed me to be a part of their sales team. As I mention in this book, having gone through the Professional Selling Skills so many years ago, I still apply some of the principles that I have learned at the Xerox School.

I am also thankful that ServiceMaster allowed me to attend the Wilson Sales Training Program. The information gained from this course was immense.

Lastly, I am thankful that my God through His Grace redeemed me by shedding the blood of His Son to cleanse me from all unrighteousness. That has allowed me to convince (sell) people who have not accepted Jesus as their Savior to what He has done for us and what He can do for them.

INTRODUCTION

In my over four decades of involvement in the profession of selling at three major companies, all leaders in their field, I have had the opportunity to personally sell, manage a sales force, and be involved in sales training. No one man is ever able to learn on his own. We must all lean on the knowledge of people who have made a career of selling. We all learn from those who have gone on before us, as in turn, others will learn from our experiences.

During the years that I spent with Sears, I learned how to sell a tangible product in a situation in which the customer came to our stores and we very quickly learned how to identify what their needs were, then helped them find the goods that fit those needs. While with Xerox, I received by far the most intensive and comprehensive sales training of my career. The Xerox Professional Selling Skills training program at Xerox University was second to none. And during my last thirty-four years with ServiceMaster I have gained more intangible sales experience than anyone would hope for.

As I worked for these three companies, I discovered that nothing will replace the passion of a good sales person, especially when this passion is coupled with a desire to succeed and to create opportunities for our organizations. As I undertook the project of writing this book, my only desire was to impart to those following some nuggets that can help them along the road to successful selling.

No book, classroom, or personal motivation program will ever take the place of the desire of any individual to excel in the art of selling. There are many books written on this subject. This will certainly not be the last of them.

Joe Kirday

If "No" Bothers You—*Quit!*

The sound of a tapping foot could be heard even through the closed door of the conference room where I was completing my second-to-last interview of the day. As there was only one person remaining in the lobby to talk to about the one available sales position with our firm, there was no doubt as to who the culprit was. Fortunately, the interview underway was nearly over, so the metronome-like tapping— which, over the previous thirty minutes, had taken on the character of Chinese water torture—would not continue long. As I saw my interviewee to the door of our second-floor office, she glared at the gentleman whose foot tapping had already put a sour taste in both our mouths, although neither of us had met him.

As I closed the door, I turned back to the suited gentleman who sat alone with his back to a window, which overlooked the parking lot. I proceeded to interview this gentleman, and against my better judgment, I hired him for the open sales position. He failed in less than a month due to his inability to stay in control and his inability to accept the "No's" that came his way. Patience is a virtue and the tapping of his foot was a clear signal of his potential failure.

In my many years of interviewing literally hundreds of sales people, one of the questions that I have always asked the prospective sales person was, "Do 'No's' bother you?"

To my amazement, I have yet to hear even one person who has said to me, "I don't like to hear 'No'."

As with example above, failure can occur in a matter of but a few weeks following the hire if the new sales person becomes overly discouraged by hearing multiple "No's." No one likes to be rejected. Not you or me. It's in our nature to want to be liked, to want to be well received by others, whether personally or professionally. The bottom line is, we like to hear "Yes." "No" hurts our feelings. It makes us uncomfortable, and we feel rejected. Most of us know from the dating scene what it's like to be turned down. Sales are no different.

Why is it that we will spend our days reading anything and everything we can get our hands on to make us better sales people (in our attempts to find the ever elusive secret of becoming a twenty-first-century sales guru) but we will utterly fail to actually believe in and put into practice even half of what we read? For instance, it is a well-known fact that for every six to seven "Yes's" you finally receive, you must inevitably go through a hundred "No's." We know instinctively that not everything we touch will turn into gold (no one is a King Midas in sales), and yet we launch into each new week with the expectation that this time-honored sales statistic will somehow be suspended in our case.

The fact of the matter is that the few gold nuggets that we do get will be worth all of the rejections we've had to endure. You've heard it before, but the pain of rejection causes it not to sink in: selling is a numbers game. Success in the sales dictionary is spelled "p-e-r-s-i-s-t"! Your commitment to persistence must overrule your natural emotional responses to the numerous "No's" you will receive.

If "No" bothers you, perhaps ditch digging would be a more fruitful endeavor. At least at the end of your work day the hole that you've dug will earn you a few dollars. It would be better for you to be a successful ditch digger and be happy than to agonize over the fact that rejection is your constant companion.

"No" today may mean "Yes" tomorrow if you are persistent. You just need to stay the course.

If You Are Going to Sit, Sit Aggressively

The other day, I got an e-mail from a franchise owner who I have worked with for over four years. In the e-mail the person said to me that "they never have gotten leads from the Home Office." That same owner copied a few of his friends on that e-mail. One of them replied to this owner, saying that "if you are waiting to build your business from the leads sent to you from the Home Office, you might as well close your doors and call it a day." He went on to say that "if you want to build a business, then get off your duff and get to working on your marketing and sales activities." How true that statement is.

We are always waiting for someone to call us. If you are aggressively waiting for the phone to ring, good luck—it will not happen. You can take my word on that. I have seen those who waited for their phone to ring end up in despair and ruins. I have also seen some people in small markets build a multimillion dollar business. The glaring difference was that one sat on his duff, while the other went out and made it happen. If selling is waiting on the phone to ring, then we all could be successful sales people and millionaires at that.

Marketing is an essential part of selling. We need to create a marketing and sales plan and then follow that plan, making adjustments as we go along.

Features Tell—Benefits Sell

In the course of the sales cycle, we are all very good at pointing out the features of our product or service. We know our product very well, and we think that the features of our product will make the sale. Unfortunately, that will never happen. People buy benefits, not features. They buy products and services that will make them feel better about themselves.

A feature is what the product or service does. A benefit is what the product or service will do for the customer. A benefit gives peace of mind, comfort, security, and the realization that the buyer made the right decision.

A benefit will allow the buyer to contribute to the greater good of his organization or his family. For example, the Volvo is known for its safety, which is a feature. Its benefit would be that the buyer is assured that, if an accident takes place, his family is secure and safe. It affects the wellbeing of the driver and the car occupants.

On a recent trip to Saint Simon Island, my wife and I stopped by a Chick-fil-A. Now every Chick-fil-A sells an excellent chicken sandwich, however, this one did not just sell the sandwich but went over and above the call of duty of making us feel welcome. The order was taken promptly; the tray was brought to our table; fresh flowers were placed at our table; mints were passed out; and the manger took time to stop by our table twice to replenish our drinks and to ask us how our meal was. As we were leaving, this manager was at the door thanking us for visiting his establishment and asked us to come back. The experience was so outstanding that I wrote Chick-fil-A an e-mail praising this store and commending the manager on running an outstanding operation. Yes, our hunger was satisfied, but more than that we felt welcomed, taken care of, and more importantly we felt that we got not just food for our bodies but also a lift to our spirit after a long trip from Atlanta.

Now here is a benefit that hit a home run. They fed us well, that is for certain. However, it made us feel good about our experience.

NEED-BASED SELLING SELLS

So many of us assume that we know what our prospect needs. We don't uncover what they are truly looking for. We make assumption during our sales process. To do that is fatal. We have to ask the right kinds of questions if we are to find out what the prospect's needs are.

You need to ask questions such as:
- *Please, share with me what is happening today in relation to the product or service that you are trying to sell.*
- *How long have you owned this current product or service?*
- *How long have you had this service?*
- *How long have you been with your current service?*
- *How much time do you spend managing this product or service?*
- *If you could, how would you improve on this product or service?*
- *What will make you change?*

And so on.

As you ask these questions, you will begin to uncover needs. Once that is accomplished, then you can fit what your company has to offer with what the customer needs. Until that takes place, your product or service will appear to be the same as everyone else's product and service, and the customer will have no reason to make any changes, especially if he perceives that you have no clue how you can help them.

Now, a sales person has to believe that his product has a unique benefit that would fit the customer's needs. If you don't, then going further will be a waste of both your prospects time and yours.

VALUE MUST BE PERCEIVED FOR
THE SALE TO BE RECEIVED

Years ago, I was making a sale proposal to a prospect. I realized that most of the time a prospect looks first for the price section of any proposal. Sure enough this prospect was no different from any other prospect; he started to look for the price section. In anticipation, I was somewhat smart, and I had taken the price section out of the three-inch-thick three-ring binder. So, I told the customer what I had done and told them that I would like for them to pay attention to my proposal and not be distracted by the price information.

After I had finished making the proposal, I handed the prospect the price portion and all I could hear from the key decision maker was, "You must be kidding me. Why so expensive?"

I asked the prospect, "Do you agree that things of value tend to cost more?"

The prospect said, "Well, I agree with that, but not that much more."

So, I offered to have the prospect to go through the proposal one more time to see what area they would like to be eliminated in order to reduce the price. The prospect said to me that he didn't want anything eliminated, and that he liked what he had heard. So, I took a calculated risk and said to the prospect that he and I had gotten to his office at the same time and that I had seen the expensive car that he was driving. Then, I asked the prospect the reason that made him buy that car. The prospect went into the many reasons why he bought that car.

At that point I said, "And then you agree with me that things of value tend to cost more."

I made a $ 1.2 million sale that day.

When people understand value, they are willing to pay the few extra dollars. If your prospect does not understand value, then regardless of how much or how little your product or service costs, it will always be too high.

SELL TO THE MOST IMPORTANT
CUSTOMER FIRST—*You!*

Years ago, I worked for a company that was the leader in its field. I had gone through the best sales training that a sales person can ask for. When the training was over, I was assigned my territory, given the sales materials that I needed, and sent on my way. For over a year and a half, I did somewhat well. However, I found out that my heart was not in that type of sales. The company had missed the boat and ignored the immerging market for small copiers and duplicators, and I began to find myself not telling the truth in order to make the sale. So I quit.

The new company that I went to work for had a product that was sold by many other competitors. However, I quickly realized that although there were many other sales people out there selling a similar product, the product I was selling was by far superior, offered more value, and gave the customer peace of mind when they purchased from us. I became successful and sold over $ 11.5 million in two years. If you believe in your product and you know that you will buy that product or service for yourself, then you have made the right decision.

It is very difficult to sell a product that you are not yourself sold on. How can you talk to a potential customer about anything if in fact you will not buy that product yourself?

The founder of ServiceMaster said best "If you don't live it, you don't believe it."

You have to believe in order to achieve.

LEARN FROM TYPES AND ANTI-TYPES

In my over four decades of being involved in sales and sales management, I have reported to many managers. Many of these managers were individuals who I tried to emulate. However, I did report to a few who very quickly made me realize that if I ever got myself in a position of managing a sales force that I will not exhibit some of the traits that these mangers possessed.

The "Type" sales managers are those who treat sales people with dignity and respect. They make them feel good about what they are doing, stand up for them, reward them, recognize them, and, more importantly, they don't begrudge the fact that they are making more money than the manager. A thank-you for a job well done goes a long way.

The "Anti-Type" sales managers are the ones who are always looking for the next sale, never stopping to say thank you for a sale just completed.

A sales person is the salt of his company. The old adage that "nothing happens until a sale is made" is very true. Many bean counters are so unhappy about the fact that a sales person is making so much money that they lose sight of the fact that the company they are counting beans for would not exist were it not for the sales force. You, as a sales manager must stand up for your people and get the other parts of the organization to realize that without the sales force none of them would have a job.

More importantly, make sure that you display the good character that your people want to emulate. Be the type, not the anti-type.

LEARN HOW TO TELL TIME

We, as sales people, must realize that timing is everything. If everything we touch in a sales cycle turns into gold, we would all be rich and already retired. For many of my sales calls the timing was just not right. The prospect had just bought a new service contract or bought the new product that I was trying to sell. If you are in sales, you will find out that your timing will never always be on target. However, that should not deter you. If the timing is not right with this prospect today, it could be later.

Years ago, I tried to make a sales call on an executive director of a not-for-profit organization. I tried at least once every other month for over six months, and my timing was never right. Then one day, I was standing at the receptionist desk when I heard a thud; I looked, and to the horror of everyone, someone had just dropped the toner tray next to a copy machine. I told the receptionist to tell that person to leave everything alone. I went down to my car, got a vacuum and a cleaning and spotting kit, came back, and took care of what could have been a total destruction of the carpet. The executive director saw me on my hand and knees vacuuming and blotting the carpet.

She turned to me and asked, "Are you not that pest that has been trying to see me regarding my cleaning services?"

I said that I was. She invited me to her office, and two months later we were serving that account.

Don't despair; when God closes one door, he will open another.

CORE VALUES ARE CRUCIAL

A company that has strong core values is an asset to a sales person. In my working life, I have worked for three companies. One of which had no core values whatsoever. The second did not have core values but did have a strong commitment to customer service. The third had outstanding core values

When I was with Sears, over every entrance to our stores hung signs that said "Satisfaction Guaranteed or your Money Back." We all lived by that motto, and although we knew that the customer was not right all the time, we made them believe that they were. Sears was the king of retailing when I was with them in the late 1960s and early 1970s.

The company that I am with as I write this book is ServiceMaster. During my tenure with ServiceMaster our core values have never changed:

- *To honor God in all we do*
- *To help people develop*
- *To pursue excellence*
- *To grow profitable*

These objectives have been the bedrock of who we are. We live and die by them. They are uncompromised, and I pray that they will never be changed. A company with a strong moral fiber can open the doors for a sales person.

So, if today you find that your beliefs and that of the company you are working for are colliding, then quit—you will be better for it.

Stop Whining

No one likes a whiner. Regardless if it's in our family life, church life, or work life, we all tend to shy away from whiners. I would rather be surrounded by positive-thinking people. Whiners come in all shapes and sizes. They come in all positions within the family and church circles and work circles—wives, husbands. and kids; company officers, managers, and workers; pastors, deacons, and church members. Oh, how none of us like to be around people who whine all the time

You might ask why I would bring family and church to this discussion. Well, let me explain. We are all sales people, regardless what position we have in life. A mother and father are selling their kids on character; a pastor is selling from the pulpit the plan of Salvation; a community leader is selling a concept. We are all in sales. We may not all sell a tangible product or an intangible service, but we are all selling and we are all in this together.

Ask yourself who has fed you the most in your life. I am not talking about food for your body but for your character, sprit, and soul. I would bet you that your answer would be the people that had the most influence on your life would be the positive people and not the whiners.

So if you happen to be one of these whiners: Stop!

You are not serving yourself well. Start your day by saying that "today I will look at life with a positive attitude and will rain sunshine on all whom I come in contact with."

Sell Relationships—Not Things

People buy from people they like, they respect, and are comfortable with. To make this point in a sales-training class I was conducting a few years ago, I made a comment that I would buy from my sister faster than I would buy from a stranger. I went on to explain that since I trust my sister that I would be more comfortable buying from her than I would be from a stranger. A hand went up in the back of room, so I asked if that person had a comment. The participants said that she would not buy a box of matches from her brother. I asked to why not? She said because she did not trust him. I thanked her for making the point for me.

You need to build a relationship with your prospect as fast as you possibly can. The sales person that breaks through that glass ceiling will be the one to make the sale. Try to find things that are in common between you and the prospect: family, hobbies, sports, trips, or common friends. We used to call it "breaking the ice." Forget that. I am talking here about building relationships. For once, who cares about the ice? Do me a favor— forget the ice until you get home. Then, you can get a glass full of ice and have some tea on me.

A sales person was trying to build relationships with a prospect, so when he was invited to sit down, this sales person looked around trying to see how he could "break the Ice." He saw a picture of a family framed and sitting on the prospect's credenza.

So, he asked, "Is that a picture of your family on your credenza?"

The customer replied. "No, it's not. I was at Wal-Mart last night. I saw this frame. it had a picture of this nice family, so I bought the frame and put it on my credenza trying to help you break the ice."

Of course it was a picture of his family—why would it be there otherwise?

A better comment would have been, "I see that you have three kids, and so do I."

Then, talk about the kids for a while. A word of caution is in order here. You will not have a lot of time to build relationships. Remember you are there to discover the customer's needs and recommend solutions that could meet those needs.

GET RID OF YOUR SALES OFFICE

Most sales people will not enjoy reading this chapter, so if you are one of them, then skip to the next chapter.

Most time is wasted by sales people sitting behind a desk in a cube or in an office. That's not where the prospect is sitting. If you are to be making sales, then get out and meet people, join organizations that can help you network, and become involved. One sales person I worked with spent more time in the office than he did out selling, and the results were evident. Sometimes, sales people hide behind their desks because they are not cut out for the job. Move them to another responsibility or another company altogether.

While we are on the topic of staying out in the field selling, working hours should not be used to fill out reports. It's a waste of time to do that. A sales person needs to do the paper work and expense reports after hours and on weekends. Working-week daylight hours are to be used selling and not doing paper work.

I told you that you won't like this chapter, but that is okay. I hope that I convinced you to stop wasting time and to get out and start selling. Your money and your company's revenue will not come from sitting behind the desk. So get off your duff and get out there where you can earn your keep.

SELL *ONLY* ON DAYS THAT END WITH A "Y"

I was traveling back to Atlanta from Charlotte, North Carolina, on a Friday afternoon. I knew that I would drive by a plant of a prospect who had not agreed to see me for the past nine months. I took a chance and called my contact and told him that I was about thirty to forty minutes away from his plant and that I was driving back to Atlanta from week-long, sales-related activities in the Charlotte market. I asked my contact, the plant manager, if I could stop and see him for about twenty to thirty minutes.

He said to me, "Don't you want to get home?"

I said to him that, if he was willing to see me, that I would stop by. He asked me to come on in and visit with him.

I got to his office at 3:30 PM. After some relationship-building conversation, I was invited to sit down. I took my watch off laid it at the corner of his desk and said to my prospect, that since I had requested twenty to thirty minutes of his time I will honor my time commitment. Then, I proceeded to ask him some direct questions about what was going on in his plant as far as cleaning was concerned. After spending fifteen minutes listening to him, I then began to talk about what my company could do to meet his needs and what my company could offer him and how we could improve the quality of housekeeping while at the same time reducing the cost. At thirty minutes, I stopped in mid-sentence and I told my contact that my time was up. He asked me to stay. Our meeting lasted for two hours. Three months later, I had a million dollar plus sale.

As our relationship continued to grow over the course of the sales cycle and beyond, I asked John why he bought from me? He referred to that day when I was willing to stop by on a Friday afternoon to make my sales pitch. He told me that most people would rather have continued on their journey home to be with their family than make one more sales call. He also told me that frankly, he had some time to kill, so he thought that he would kill that time listening to a hungry sales person.

Friday afternoon is a great time to sell. Most other sales people have called it a day. So you might as well be there to meet with a prospect. Any day that ends in "y" is always a sales day. You will never know who you may come in contact with that could be a future customer. Prospects come from all walks of life.

Also, please remember the three-foot rule of selling: If you are within three feet of anyone, introduce yourself, tell them briefly what it is that you do, give them your business card and offer your services.

You potential customer may be lurking anywhere.

Name-Dropping Is Good

Years ago, my wife and I were having a Sunday School gathering at our house. Mike, an acquaintance in my class came, and he and I were standing at our deck talking and getting to know each other a little better. Mike asked me what I did, and I asked him what he did and he told me that he worked for Freightliner. My eyes just about popped out of my face. I asked him if he knew Richard L. (true story but not the real name of the plant manager). Mike told to me that Richard and he play golf once a week and that they are very close friends. I told Mike that I had been trying to see Richard at their plant in North Carolina to no avail. Mike asked me to call Richard the following Monday and go through my same routine. Mike also told me that if I get the same reaction to mention his name to Richard.

So, the next Monday, I got to Richard and went through my same routine. Sure enough, Richard again did not want to meet with me.

So, I said to him, "By the way, Mike M. says hello."

Richard's tone changed immediately. He asked me how I knew Mike, so I told Richard that Mike attended my Sunday School class and we are friends. At his point, Richard asked me when I could come to meet with him. As in my other stories, relationships were built, needs identified, and the sale was made.

It is okay to drop names. However, please make sure that whatever name you are dropping has the following two qualifications: first, that that person has given you permission to use their name, and second that there exists a good relationship between your prospect and the person whose name you plan on using. Otherwise it will backfire.

That is why I strongly recommend that a sales person should get involved in networking groups, civic organizations, and the Chamber of Commerce. There is power in knowing people who can open doors for you.

Know Your Delusions about Communication

We all hear chatter, noise, and useless talk. Don't open your mouth and talk aimlessly. We try to communicate, and we truly think that we are getting through, only to come to a screeching halt when we realize that no one heard a word we had said. I know preachers who are so good at saying a lot and at the same time saying absolutely nothing. They spend forty minutes thinking that we heard what they had said, only to find out that as far as the congregation is concerned, they said nothing. They are so proud of themselves, yelling and screaming, that every word is lost in the translation.

Think before you open your mouth. Communication is an art that can be developed. However, you need to understand that in order for you to be able to communicate effectively with your prospect you must first listen. By listening you will then be able to communicate things of value, things that your customer wants to hear. Don't just open your mouth to rattle facts and figures when your customer has no interest in them.

When God created man and woman, he was far too wise in His creation, wiser than many would give Him credit for. He gave all of us one mouth and two ears. If God intended for us to talk more than we listen, then He would have reversed that order. Listen twice, speak once. Your prospects will appreciate you more.

TRUST IS *NOT* UNBREAKABLE

In any given sales scenario there will always be some prospects who will have reasons not to trust you. Some of these situations result from sins of commission; others are sins of omission. In either case, they are there, and you need to be aware of them.

Let's first talk about the sins of omission. I do not speak like someone who was born in the United States. I have a slight accent. I can't help it. That is who I am. If I had taken that as a hindrance, then I would not have been successful in my sales career and I would not have made a single sale in my life. Rather, I took that and turned it into strength. I realized that people are listening to me because of my accent. And because of that I was able to communicate well. Now, I am not saying that the fact that I have an accent is a sin. What I am saying is it is something that I can't change. It is what it is.

On the other hand, the sin of commission is something that I you would have created and put up as a barrier. Some of such sins are: not living up to your word; showing up late for an appointment; being unprepared; mumbling your way through your presentation; and the list goes on.

Some things we don't have any control over. Who we are, where we were born, our ethnic background, or gender, our faith—none of these should have any bearing on how we conduct ourselves during the sales cycle. In all of these situations, a sales person can capitalize on what seem to be deficits and make them strengths.

I work with a franchise owner who thinks that the only reason he does not make any sales is because he has a heavy accent. In truth, he has not made sales is because he elected to find an excuse not to.

If you want me to help you create a barrier, give me a call, I can come up with a boat load for you to make excuses with so you don't have to go out and sell.

CAVEAT VENDITOR—OR—KNOW WHO YOU ARE SELLING TO

One of the sales person's biggest mistakes is that he or she spends hours talking about the right kinds of issues only to later find that they were talking to the wrong person. It is better to find early on in the sales process if you have an audience with the person who will be making the final decision regarding your product or service. Wasting time is not in a sales person's vocabulary. With that being said, one needs to be very careful in asking the right question to make sure that the person to whom you are speaking with is not alienated.

One such correct question would be: "Who besides you will be involved in making this decision?"

That way, you keep the person that you are talking with in the loop rather than making them feel insignificant. There are a number of positions within an organization that you need to be aware of. The higher you are in the hierarchy, the better off you will be. These positions are:

The Approver

The Conqueror

The Initiator

You need to find out on your very first sales call if you are at the right level within the organization. Sometimes there may be more than one person at each of these levels.

CREATE GAPS BETWEEN THE CUSTOMER'S "HAVES" AND "WANTS'"

One of the ways to find out if you are moving in the right direction in the sales process is for you to quickly identify what the customer really wants insofar as your product and service can provide. In order to accomplish this, you must first find what the customer currently has and what he really wants. If you are able to separate these two things then you can move ever more closer to closing the sale.

As the customer begins to share what he has currently—an older car, a car too small, a car that drinks too much gas, and so on—you can start by asking what the customer wants: a newer car, a more efficient car, a larger car, and so on. From that point on, you can move him to a product or service that you have that will fit his needs.

Here is one of the best examples I know. Let us assume that you have a body temperature of 98.6 degrees. Medically do you need anything? No, what you have is what you want. What if it's 99.5? Now do you need anything? Maybe some rest and an aspirin. What if you have 101 degrees? Now you are thinking about seeing a doctor. What if it's at 103 degrees? Now you are heading to the emergency room.

The wider the gap you identify between what the customer has and what he wants, the better you can offer the prospect solutions to fit what he wants. Ask the questions that will identify what the needs and wants are, and you will be moving in the direction of making the sale.

Here I need to make one assumption, and that is what the customer wants is in fact is what you have.

By All Means—*Ask* for the Sale

In many of my sales classes I ask the following question. What percentage of sales people do you think don't ask for the sale at the end of their presentation? The answers range from 10 to 30 percent. I then say that the national statistics show that 66 percent of sales people go through the gyration of a sales presentation only to walk away without actually asking for the sale.

Sometimes asking does not only mean a signature on the bottom line. It could be asking for the next step in the sales process. Why do you think that the car dealership does not want you walking out of their showroom without you signing on the bottom line? They know through experience that if a customer walks out of their showroom that most of the time they will lose that sale.

The larger the deal, the longer the sales process will take. So, that is why I say you need to at least have the customer commit to a next step or to a follow-up meeting. If you don't, a better sales person could come right behind you and snatch that sale right out of your lazy little hands. That could happen because you didn't want to be pushy.

There is a vast difference between the "The Meek shall Inherit the Earth" and the ignorant shall have the sale slip right through their fingers. Go for it—what do you have to lose?

Don't Assume the Sale Is Over
When the Customer "Buys"

So the right questions have been asked, the needs and wants have been identified, the relationships are built, the sale is asked for, and the deal is closed—so now you think that the sales process is over. Think again.

Many a company has gone into bankruptcy not because their sales force didn't make the sales; they went broke because their backdoor was wide open. Their backdoor was like a colander—you pour water into a colander, and it goes right through it. If your company does not develop a good customer-service attitude, they may not go broke tomorrow or the day after or even the day after that. However, broke they will go. No company can sustain its growth if they are constantly losing customers.

Furthermore, the sales person's job has now become a bit harder. If a sales person is to make sales they will need good referrals. With the company losing customers right and left, where is the sales person going to get those referrals? Growth for that company will even be more difficult. For every hundred dollars lost because of poor customer service, the sales person needs to make a new hundred dollar sale just to break even. A company with no sustained growth is a company that is doomed to fail eventually.

Don't Assume the Sale Is Over
When the Customer Buys

THERE ARE ALWAYS MORE RULES
(final thoughts on selling in the twenty-first century)

When you are on stage in front of a prospect, dress the part.

Always arrive five minutes early. On time is late; early is on time; and late means the train has left the station.

It is your job to take care of the customer, although sometime it appears that they don't care about you.

Don't spend your time driving all around town. Narrow your prospect list.

If you take a prospect out to lunch, let them eat. Use this time to sell not eat yourself. Take the best seat at the table, that way your customer will have fewer distractions.

Objections will always be there. Learn how to overcome objections about your particular product or service.

Everyone you meet can be your potential next customer. Treat all people with dignity and respect.

Always return all calls that you get within twelve hours. Don't let them fester.

If you think that the answer you hear is not what you want to hear, then don't ask the question.

Trial close every step of the way.

Cold calling does work.

Create a good message that you can leave on the customer's voice mail. It should compel them to return your call.

Send a hand-written thank-you note after each time you make a contact with a prospect.

Ask for referrals.

Hand your business card to everyone you meet. They can be your next customer. It is a cheap marketing tool.

Create a thirty-second elevator speech that tells what business you are in. Remember: features tell and benefits sell.

Always realize the time spent with a customer is not an interruption to your work.

Remember the customer is what makes your company.

The customer pays your wages.

Smile when you speak with the customer, even when you are on the phone. Your voice does smile.

Never argue with the customer—you will lose.

Always be positive.

Listen, listen, listen—you may learn something

Inspect what you expect.

Give the customer more than what they are paying you for. Go the extra mile.

Make your people proud of what they are doing.

Always keep in mind how much a customer can spend with you over a lifetime.

Acknowledge your errors, say you are sorry, and fix the problems.

These are only a few suggestions—I know that you can come up with more. Always remember to make sure that the backdoor is made out of solid wood and that it is not a screen door.

CONCLUSION

The moral of this book is that we, as sales people, must always be on the lookout for sales opportunities. Unless we happen to be in a type of business in which the customers come to us, we must be constantly vigilant about our sales and marketing activities. We must not wait for the opportunity to come knocking, like the Mr. Opportunity who advertises Honda cars, but we must go after and create our own opportunity.

The road to sales success is littered with those who have gone on before us, only to give up before the journey even began. But it has also been my experience that some individuals, men and women of sales valor, have gone on to prove that, if we chase our dreams when it comes to selling, that we can find the customer. Those of us in the service industry have long learned that you can't start a business and sit on your laurels waiting for the customer to come knocking. We realized that the spoils come to those who go after them, and then and only then we will become victors in our own industry.

I encourage those who read this book to do what we read in the Bible in Isaiah 40:31 "They shall mount up with wings as eagles; they shall run, and not be weary; and they shall walk, and not faint." Our profession is a noble one, and we each have the same opportunities as everyone else.

Finally, practice, practice, practice, and when you think you have your sales presentation figured out, practice some more.

Good selling.

NOTES

NOTES

NOTES

NOTES

NOTES

ABOUT THE AUTHOR

Joe immigrated to Canada from Lebanon in 1963 and to the United States in 1967. During his undergraduate studies, Joe began working for Sears. In 1969, Joe was drafted into the U. S. Army and served as a Chaplain Assistant, while serving in the Republic of Viet Nam earning Bronze and a Silver Stars for meritorious service, and was honorably discharged in 1972. He then returned to work for Sears and completed his undergraduate work on the G.I. Bill. In 1975, Joe joined Xerox in sales for two years, after which he joined the ServiceMaster Company in 1977 and worked there in a number if management, sales, and sales management roles.

Joe has been involved in sales and the sales management functions for over forty years. He holds a Bachelor of Arts in business administration, a Master of Divinity and a Doctor of Ministry degrees. Joe is also a member of the ServiceMaster Ten Million Dollar Sales Club and is a graduate of the ServiceMaster Graduate Program.

Joe has also conducted a numerous sales training seminars in the United States, Canada, and Europe.

Joe is an ordained Southern Baptist Minister and is heavily involved in his local church.

Joe also preaches whenever the opportunity presents itself.

Joe has been married to his wife, Debbie, for forty-two years and they have two grown, married children and two grandchildren, Austin and Abbie. Joe and his family reside in the Atlanta area.

www.ingramcontent.com/pod-product-compliance
Lightning Source LLC
Chambersburg PA
CBHW021916170526
45157CB00005B/2084